This coloring book belongs to...

_____

_____

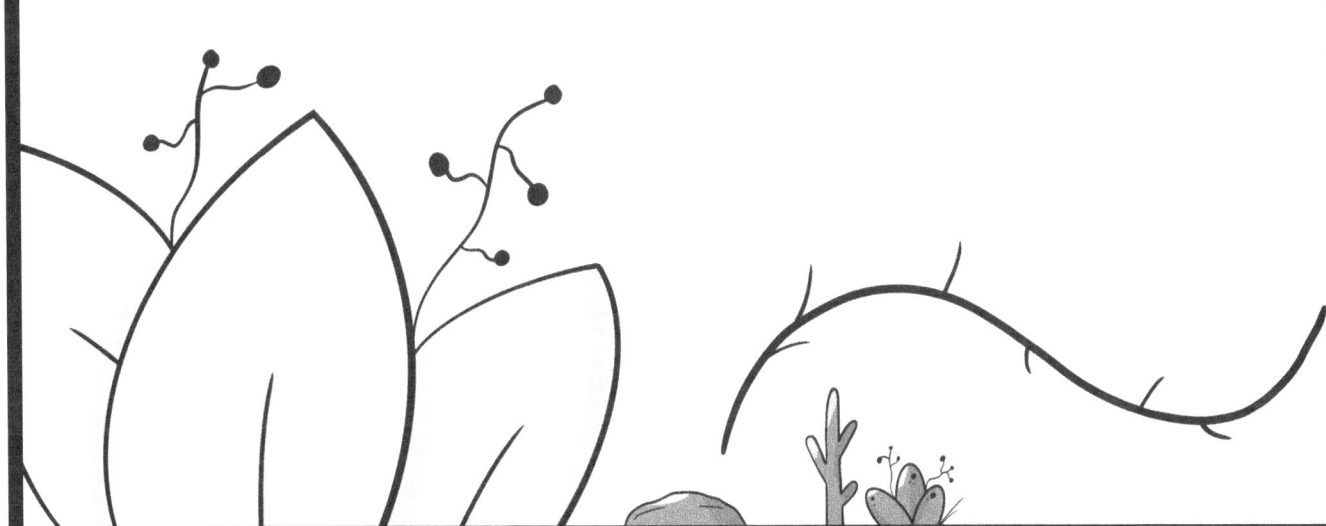

Copyright 2022 Carter Art & Designs
illustrator: Cody Carter
www.facebook.com/carterartndesign

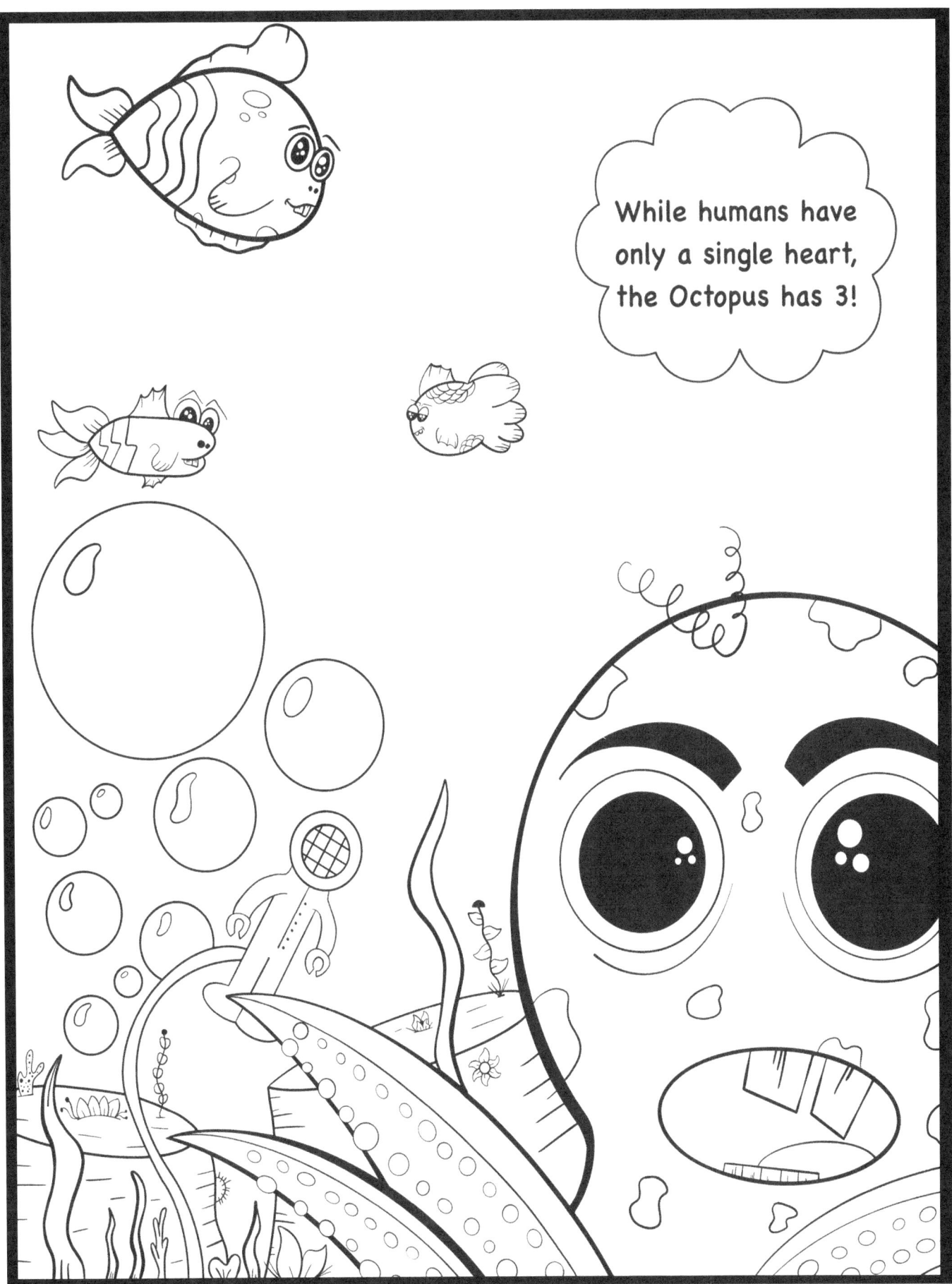

Happy Octopus

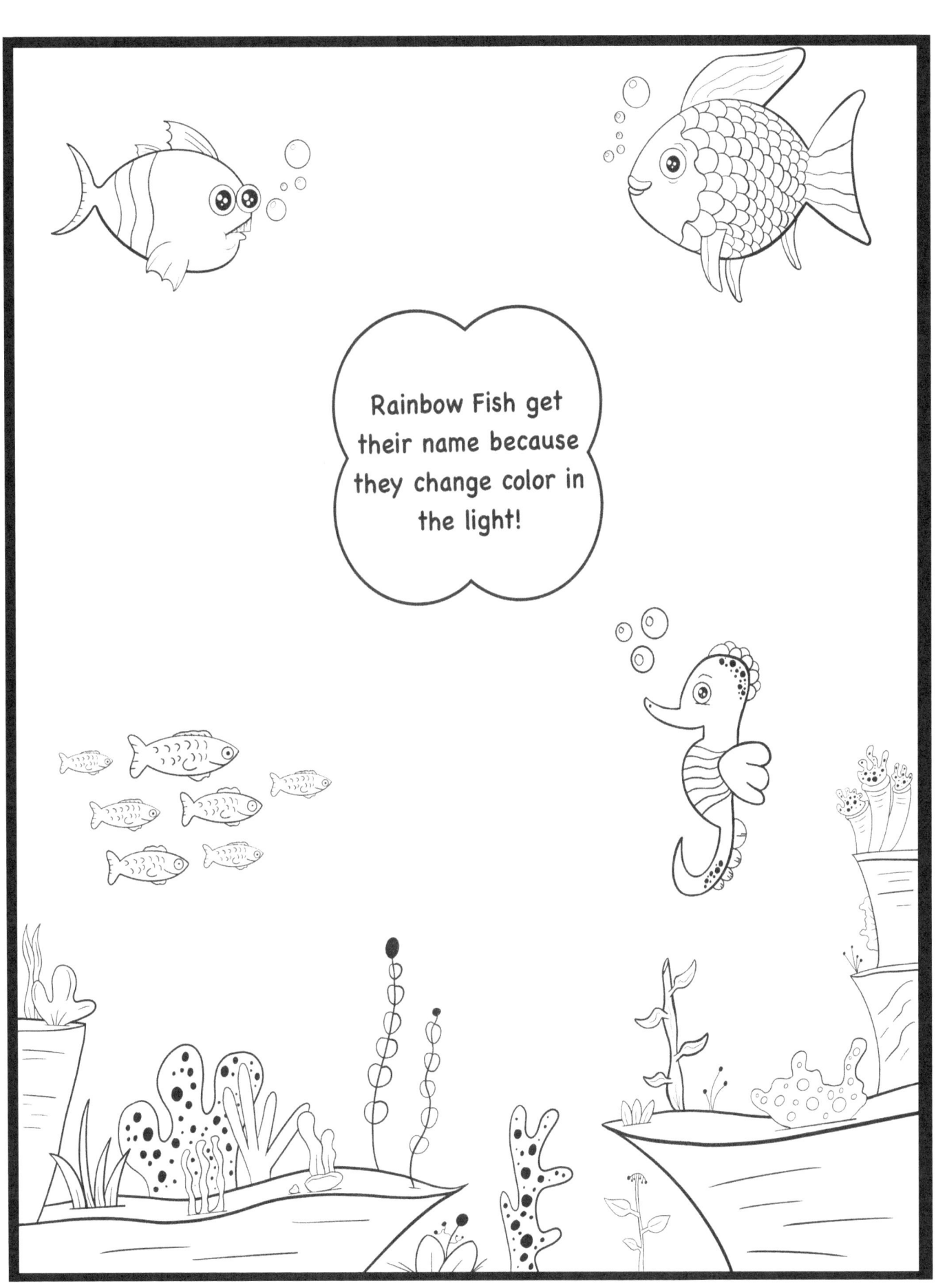

Calm Rainbow Fish

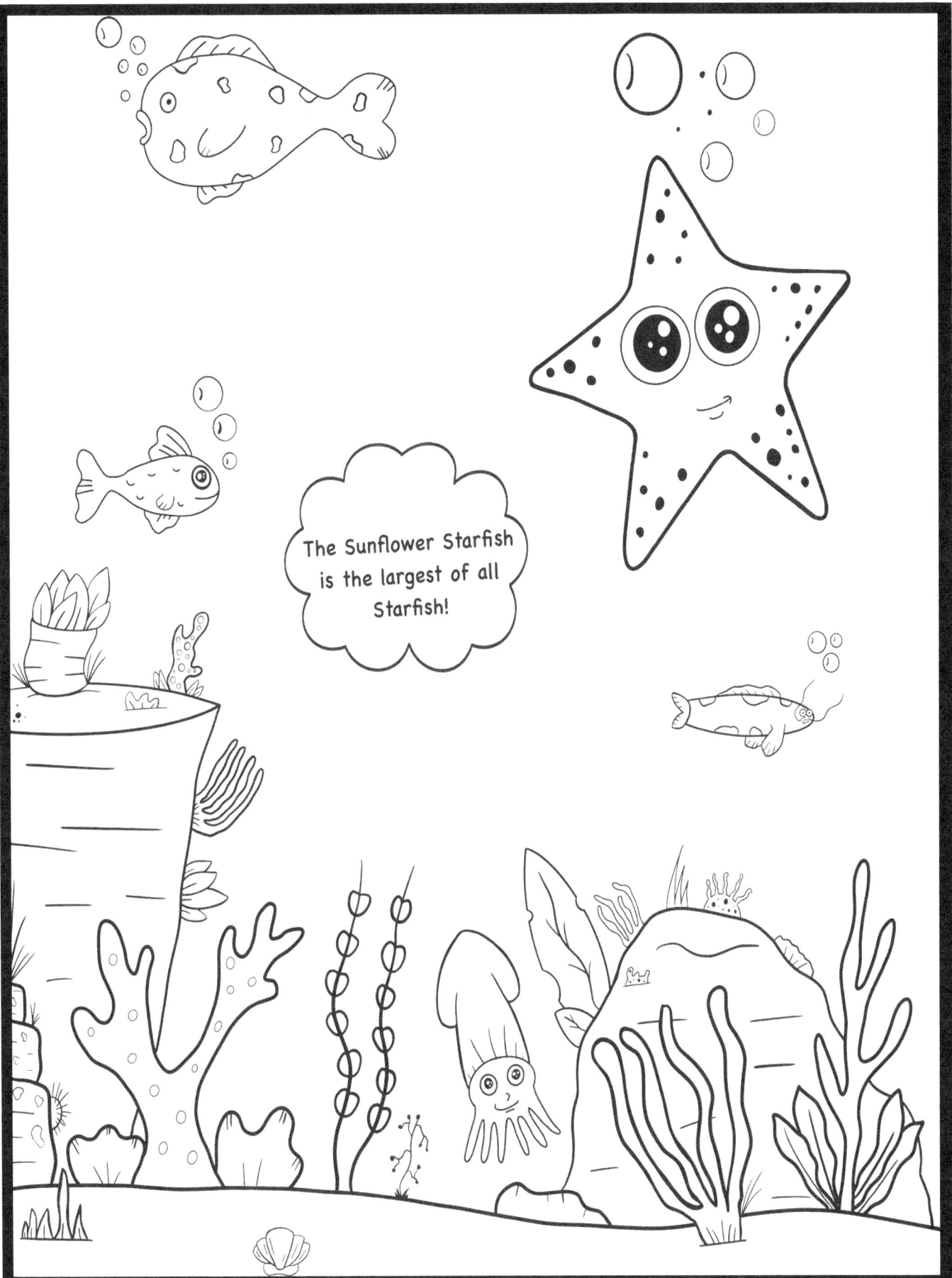

Smiley Starfish

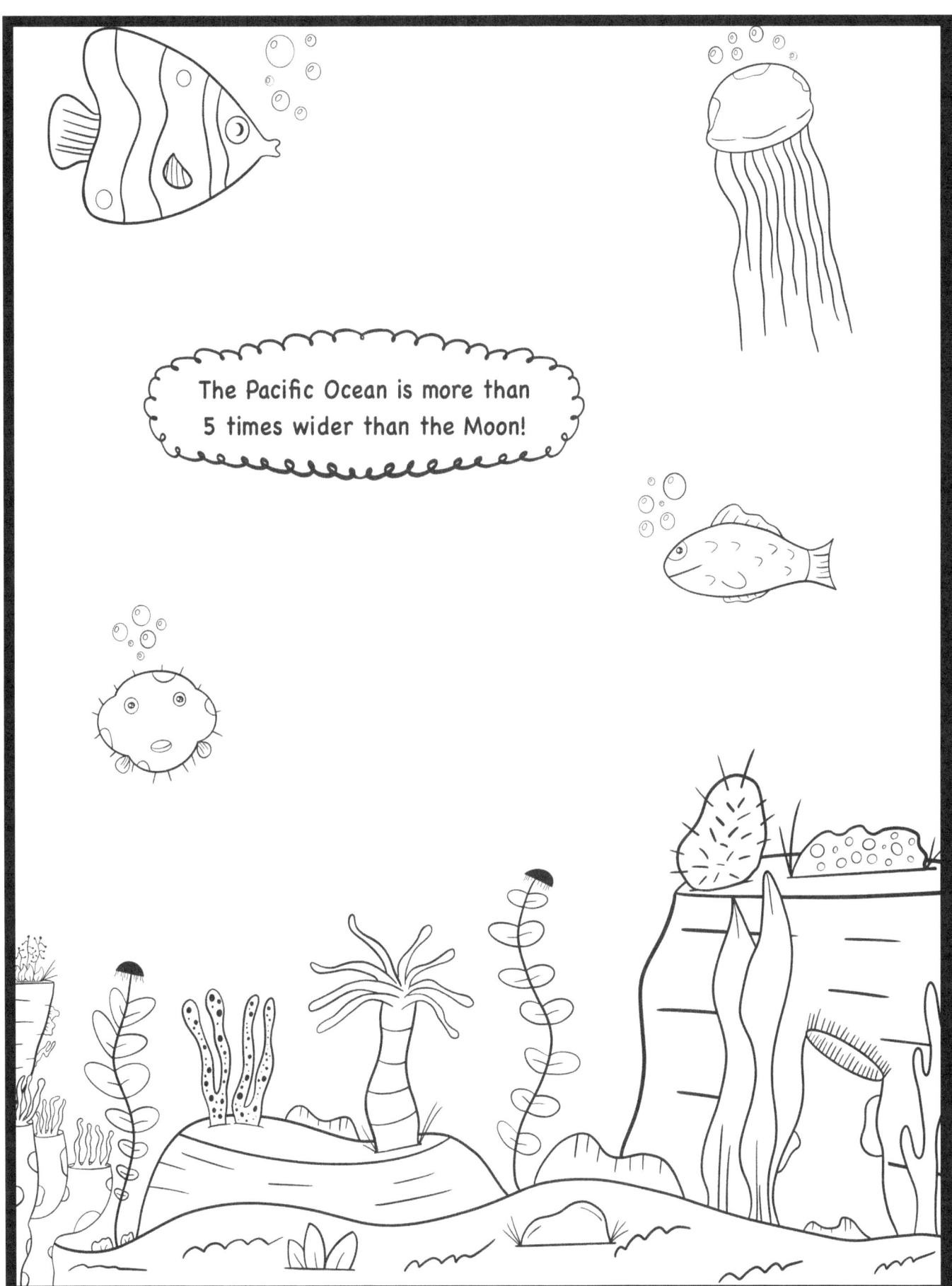

Lively Reef

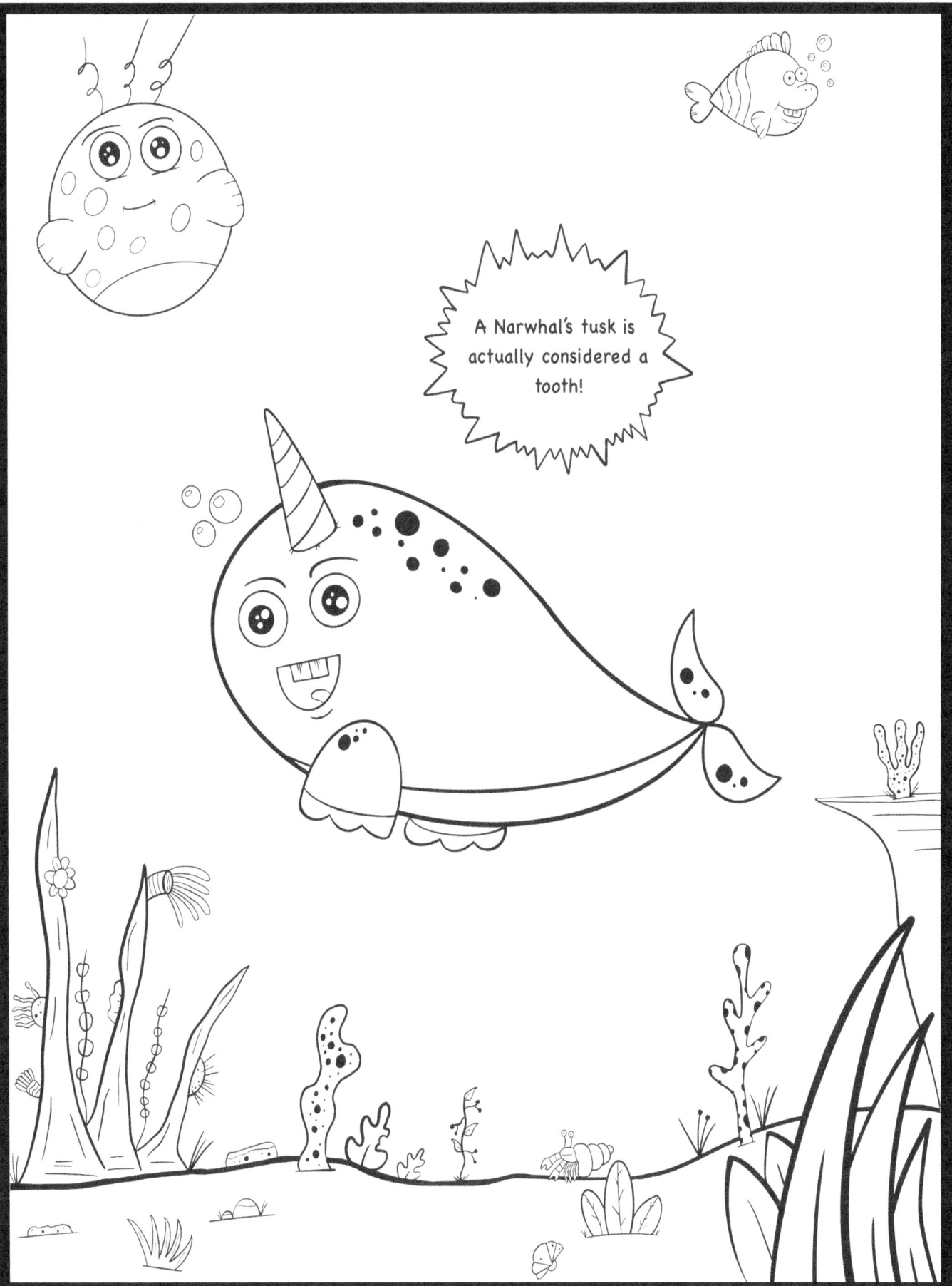

Suspicious Narwhal

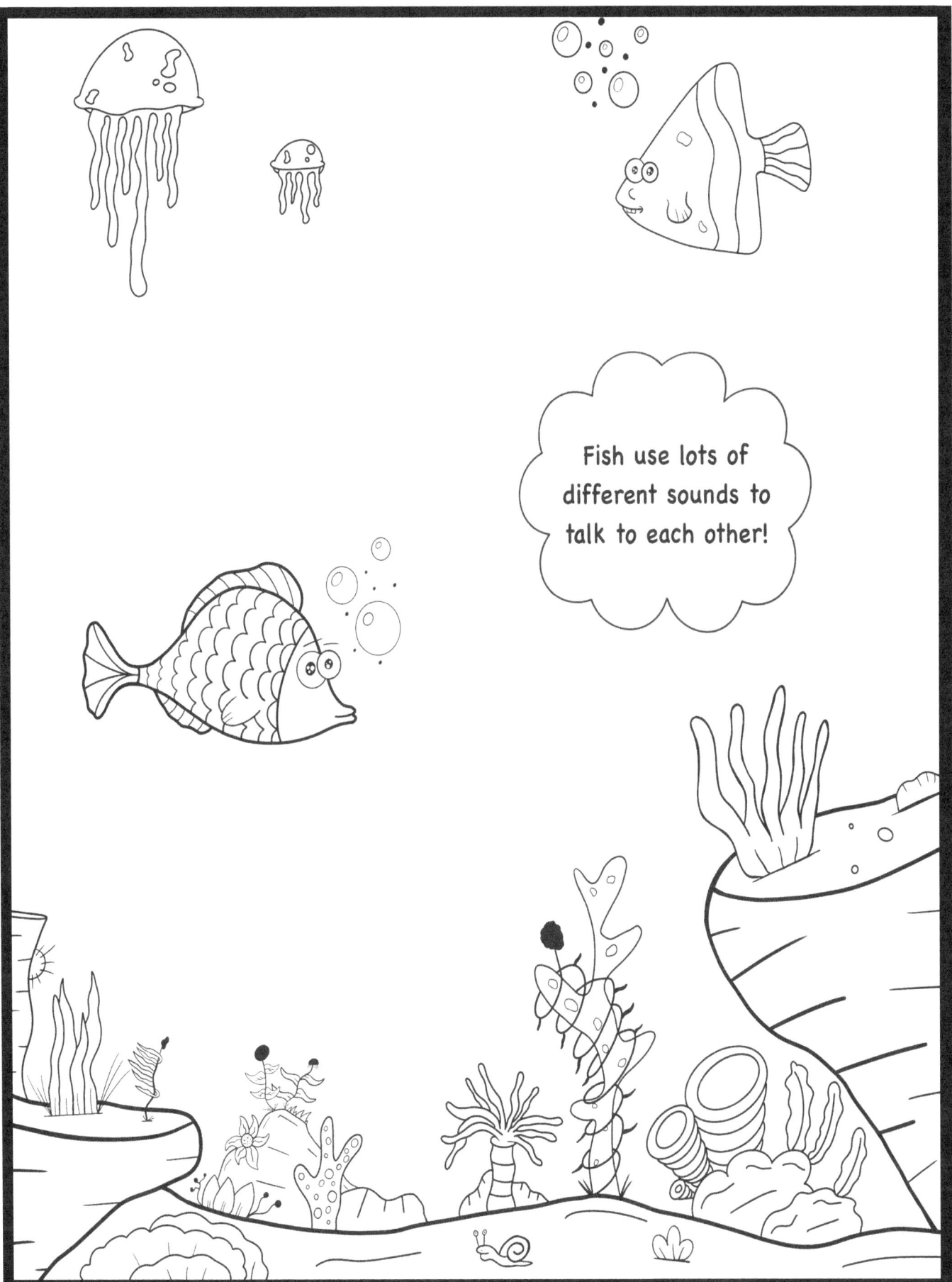

Lively Reef 2

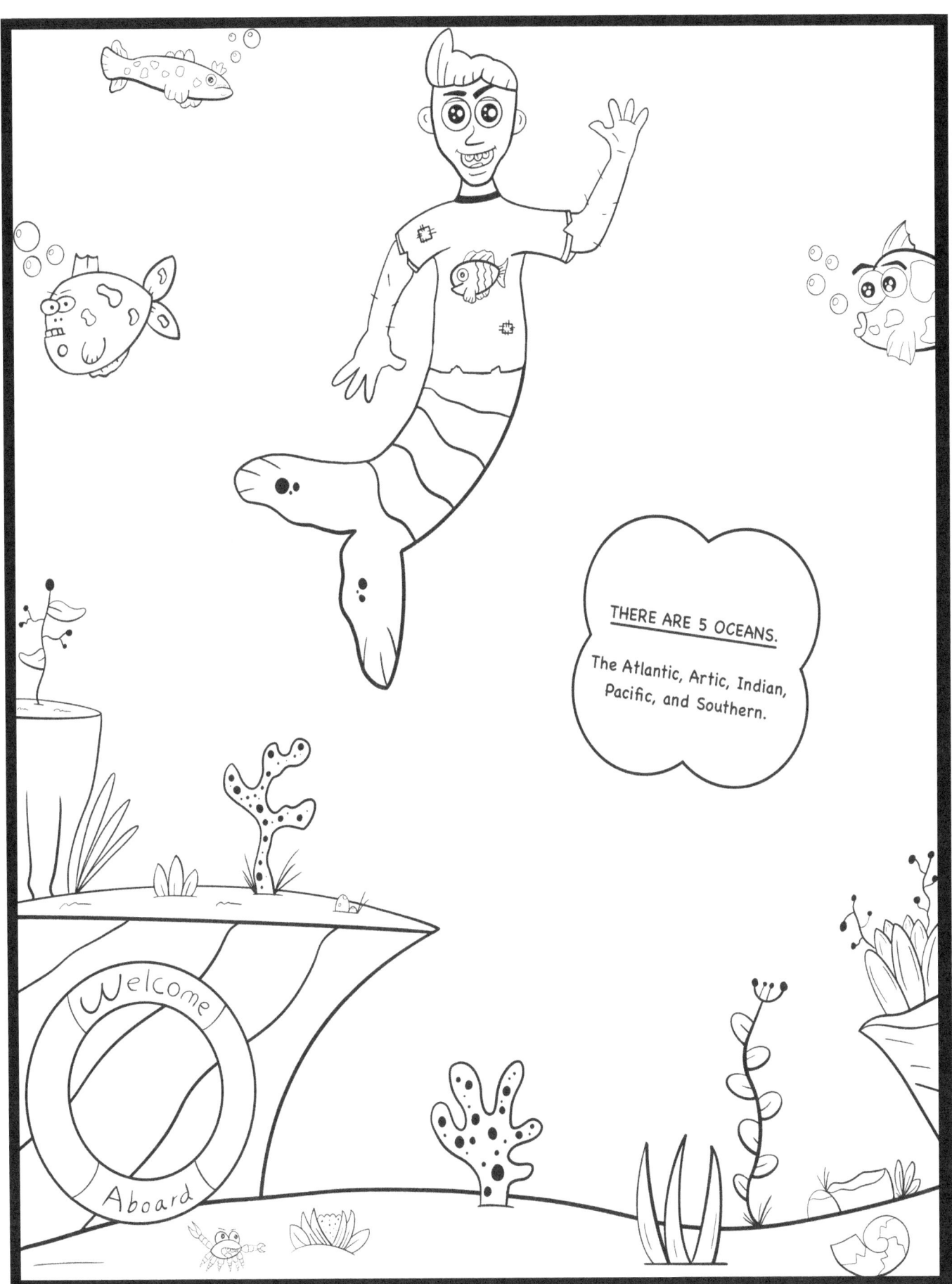

Welcoming Merman

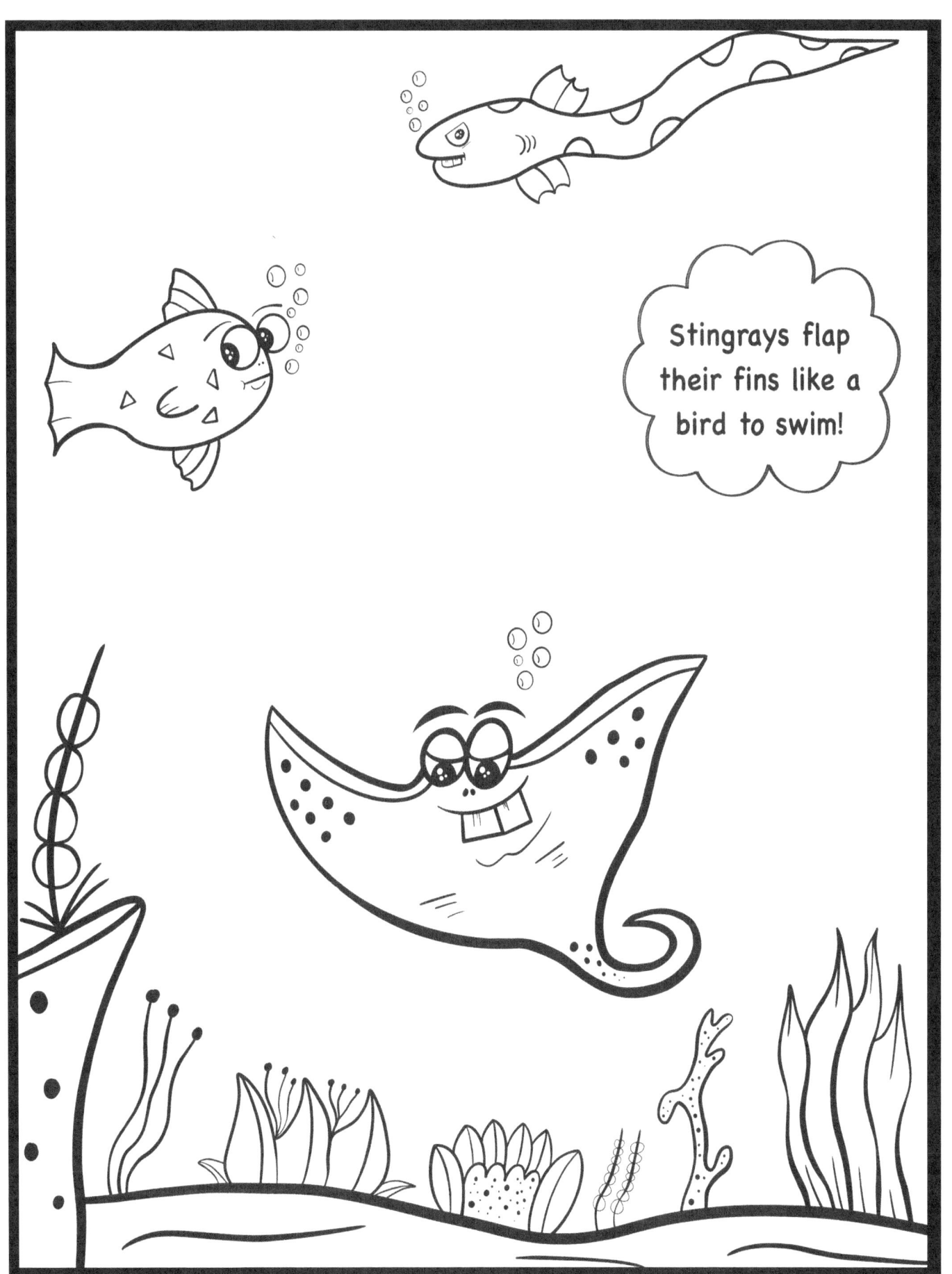

Excited Stingray

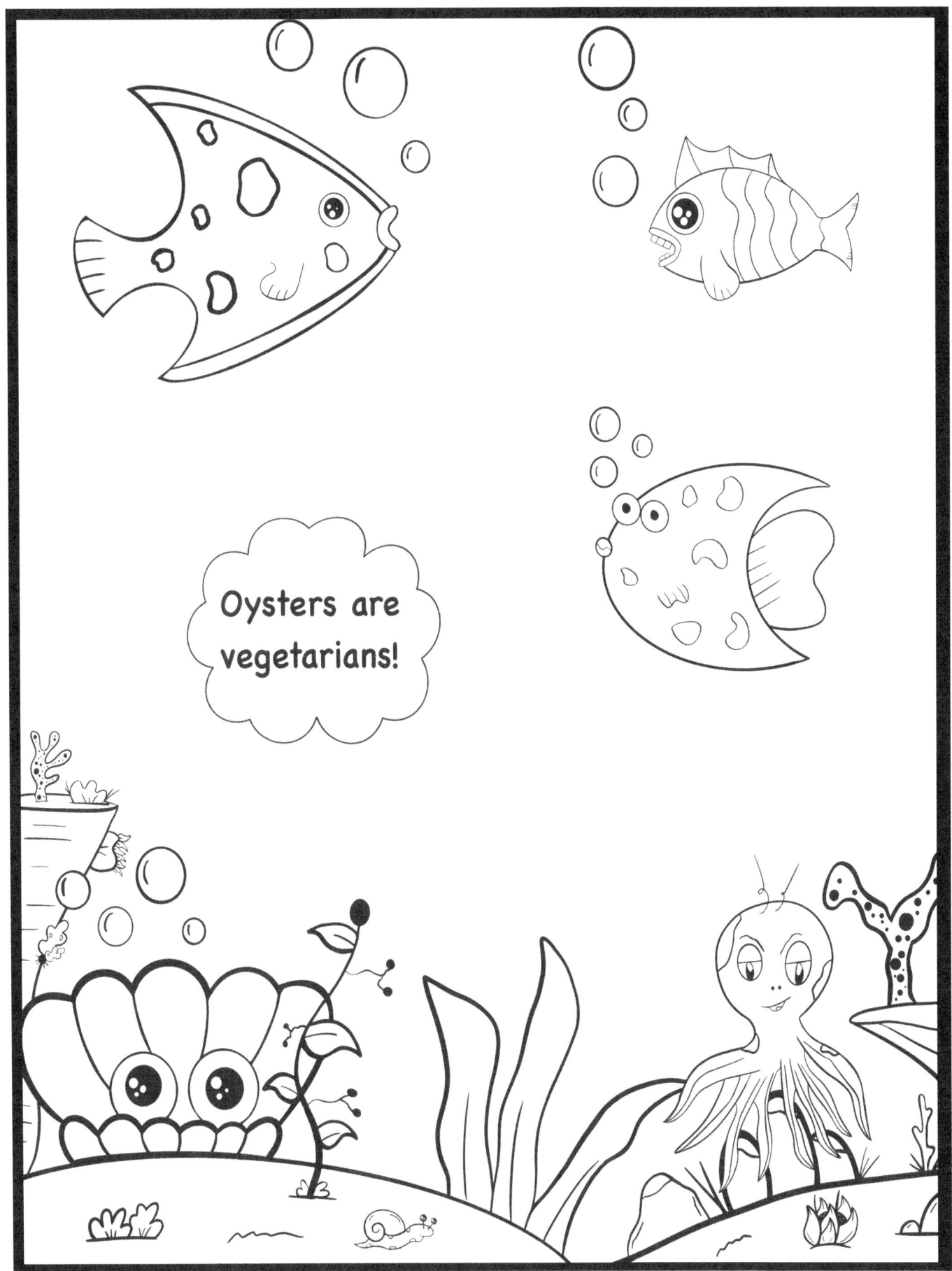

Bubbly Oyster

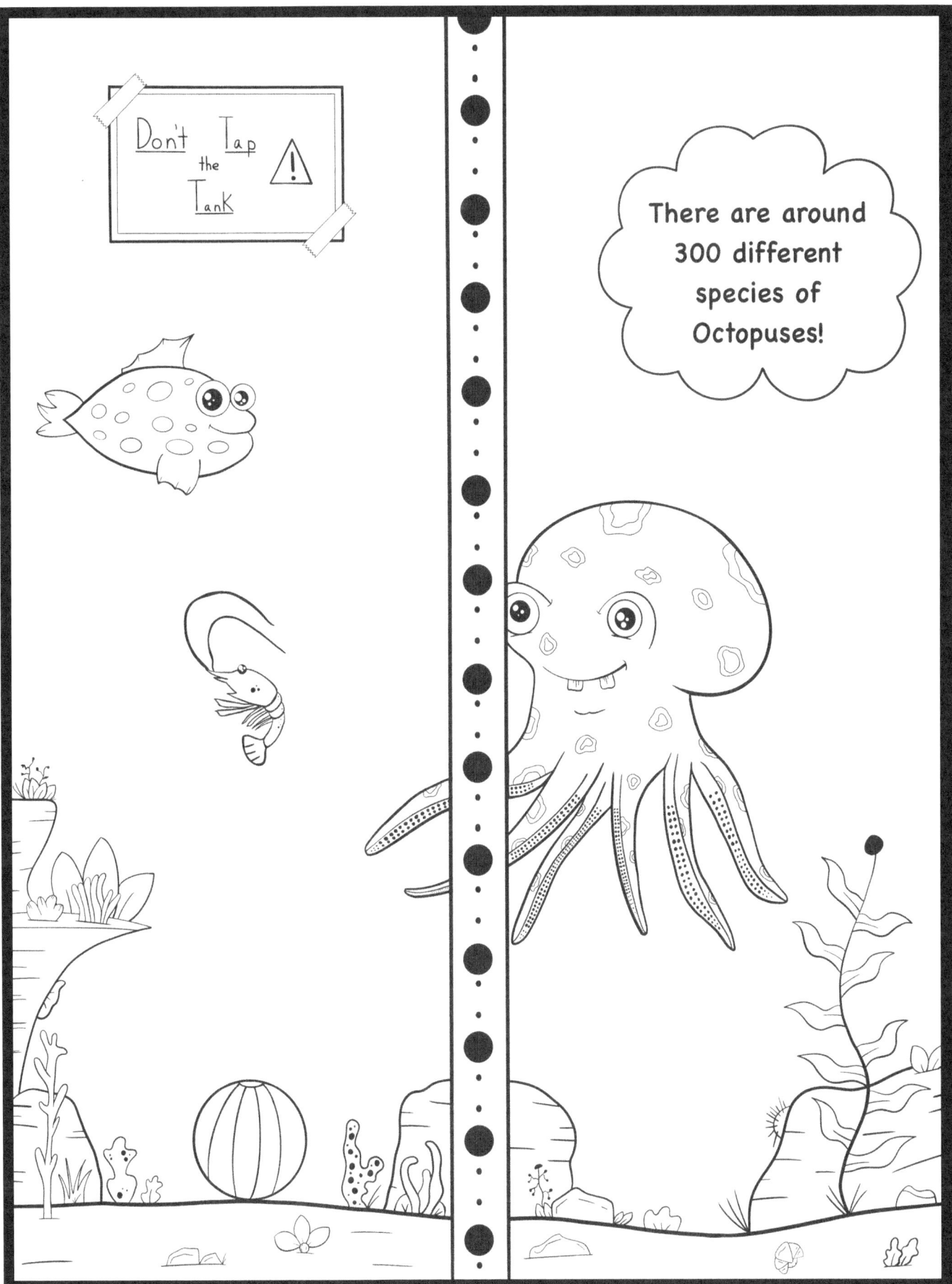

Octopus Tank

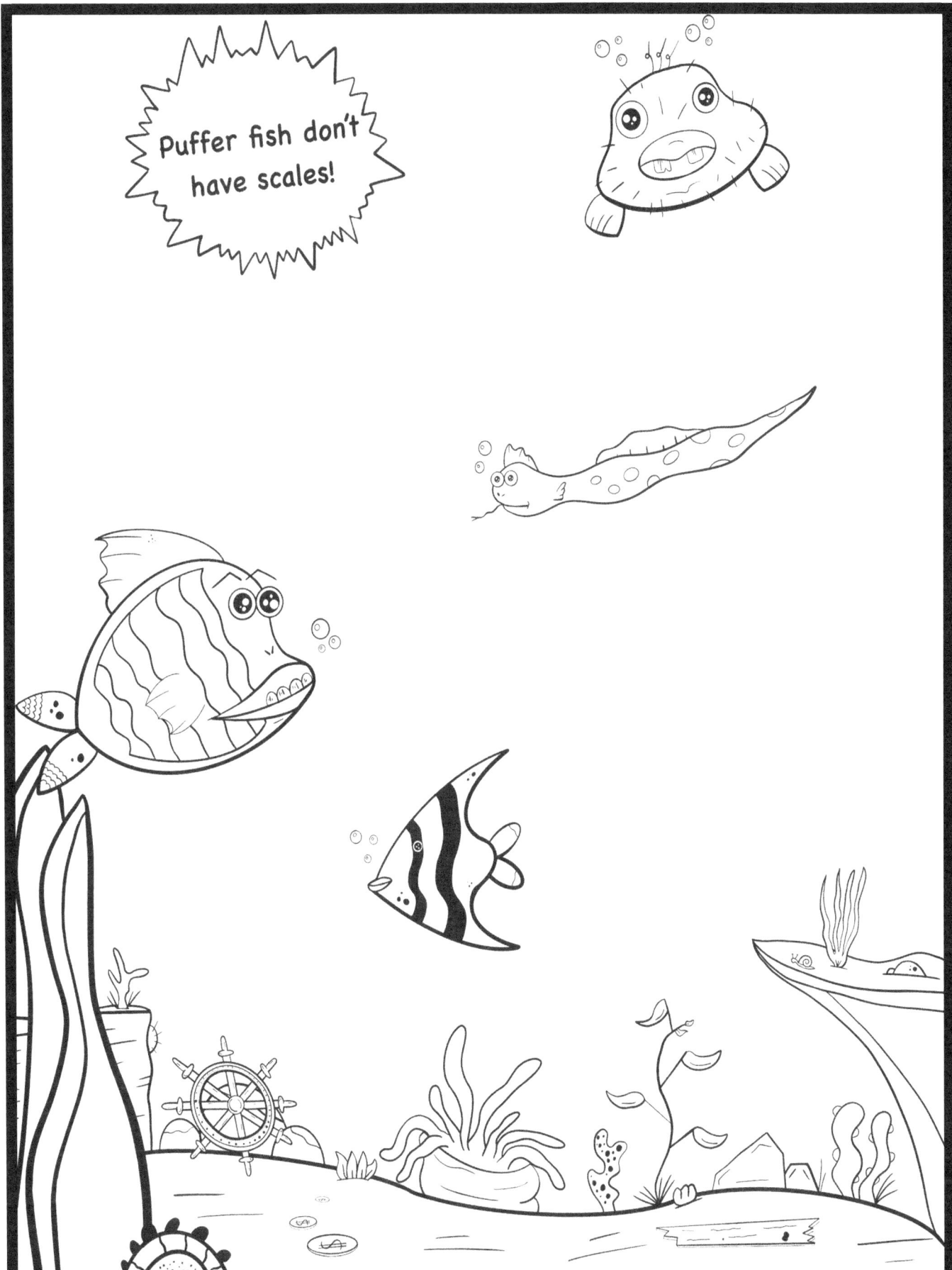

Grouchy Pufferfish

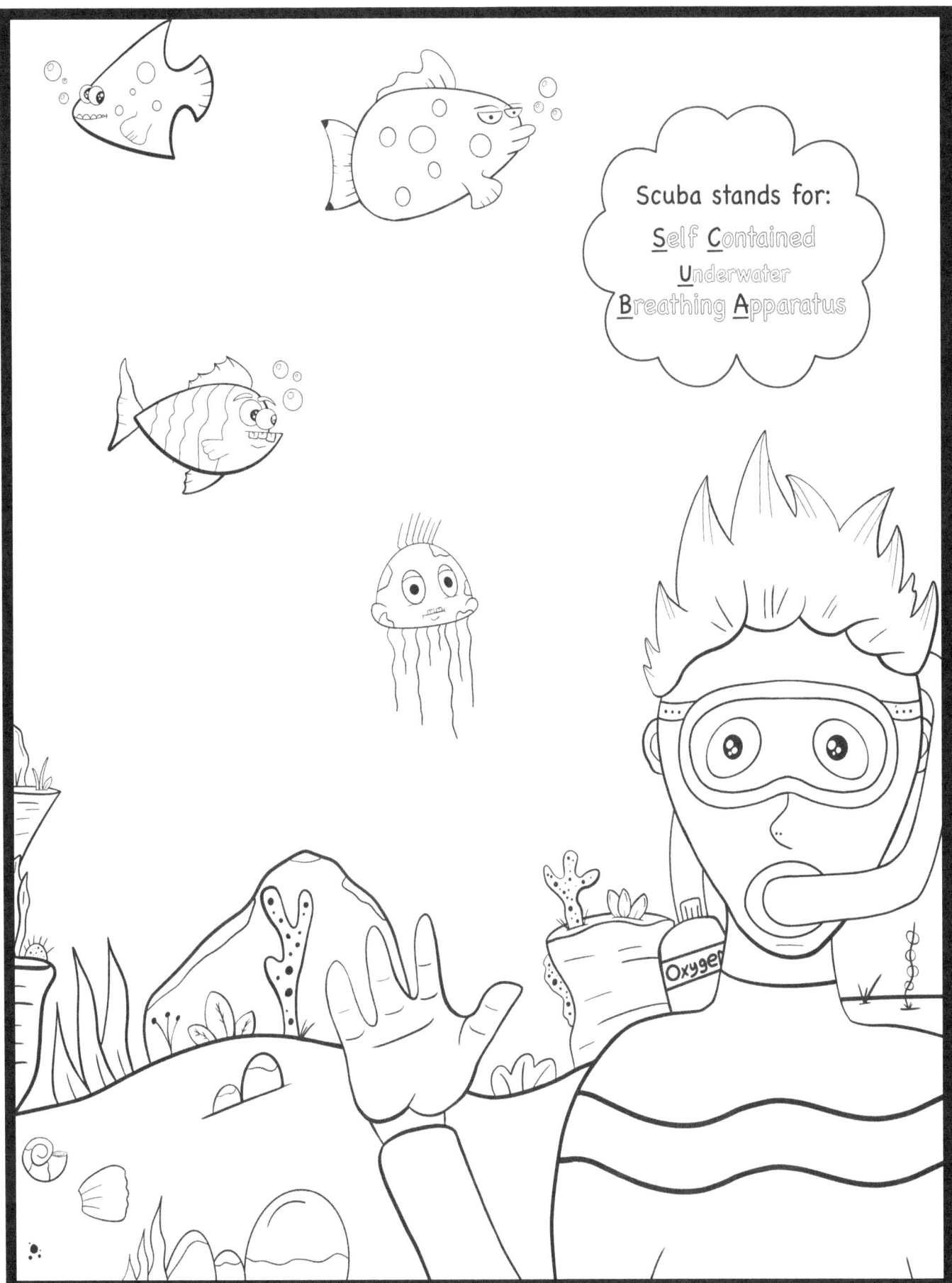

Friendly Diver

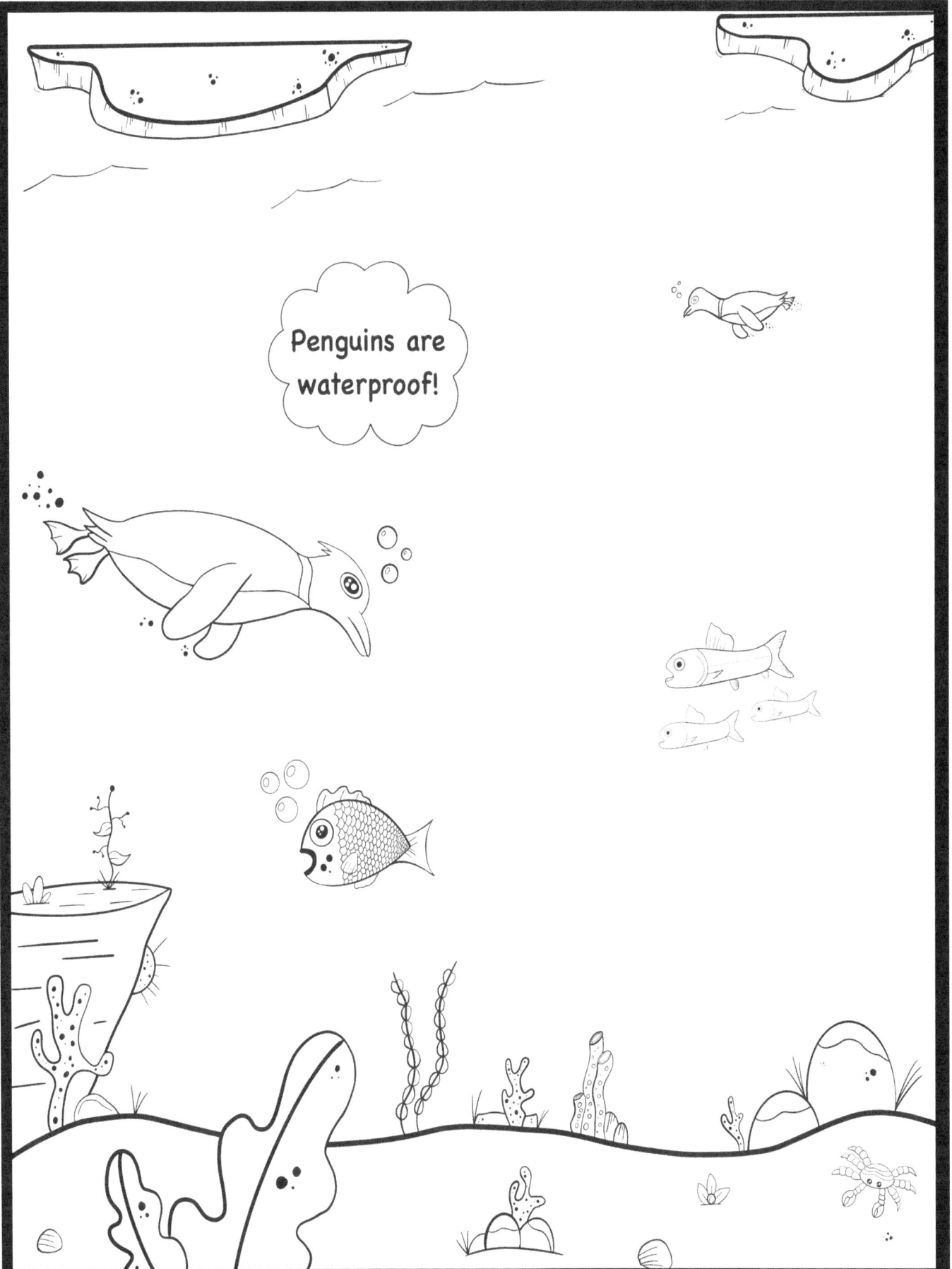

Relaxing Penguins

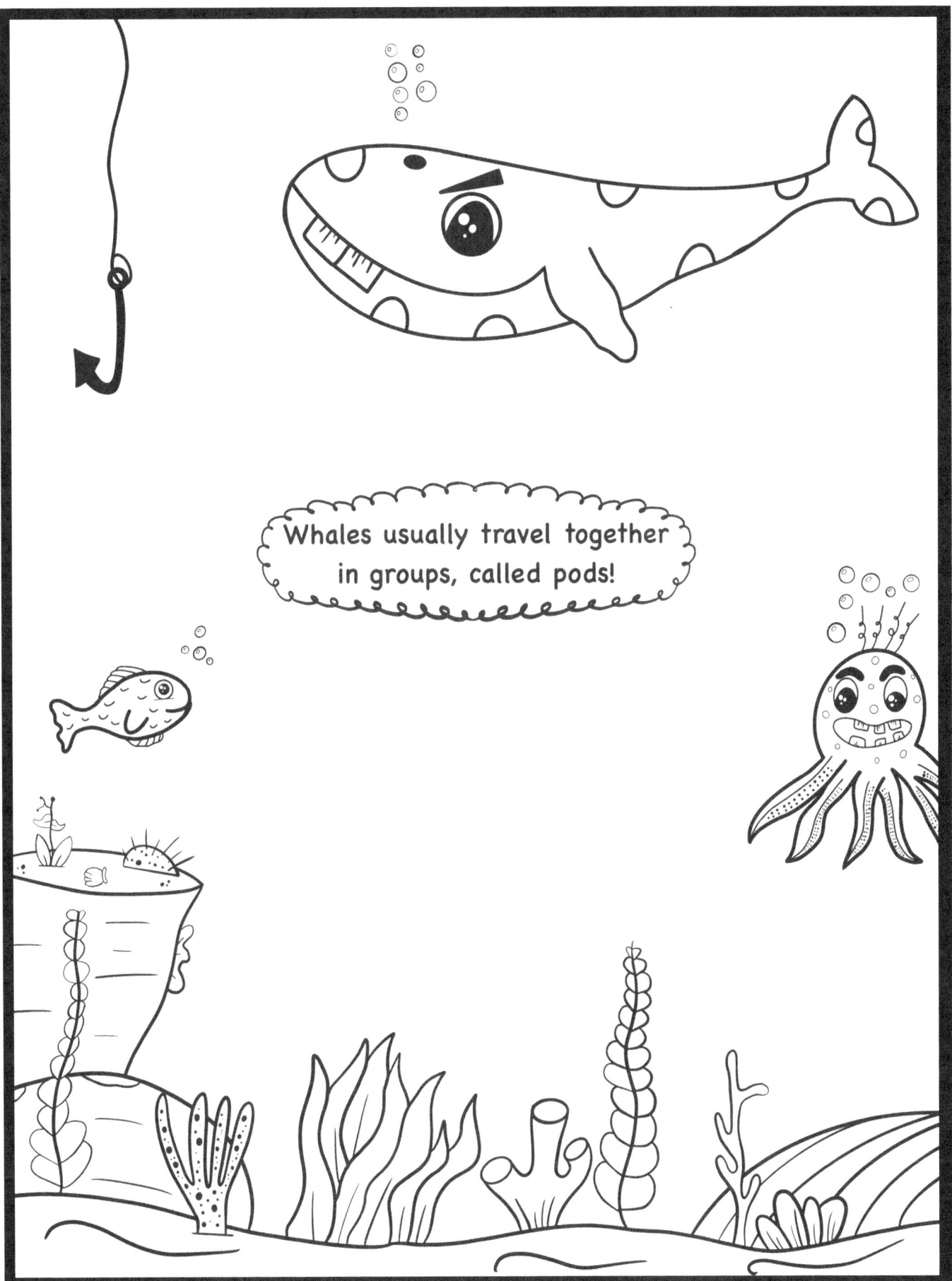

Mischievous Whale

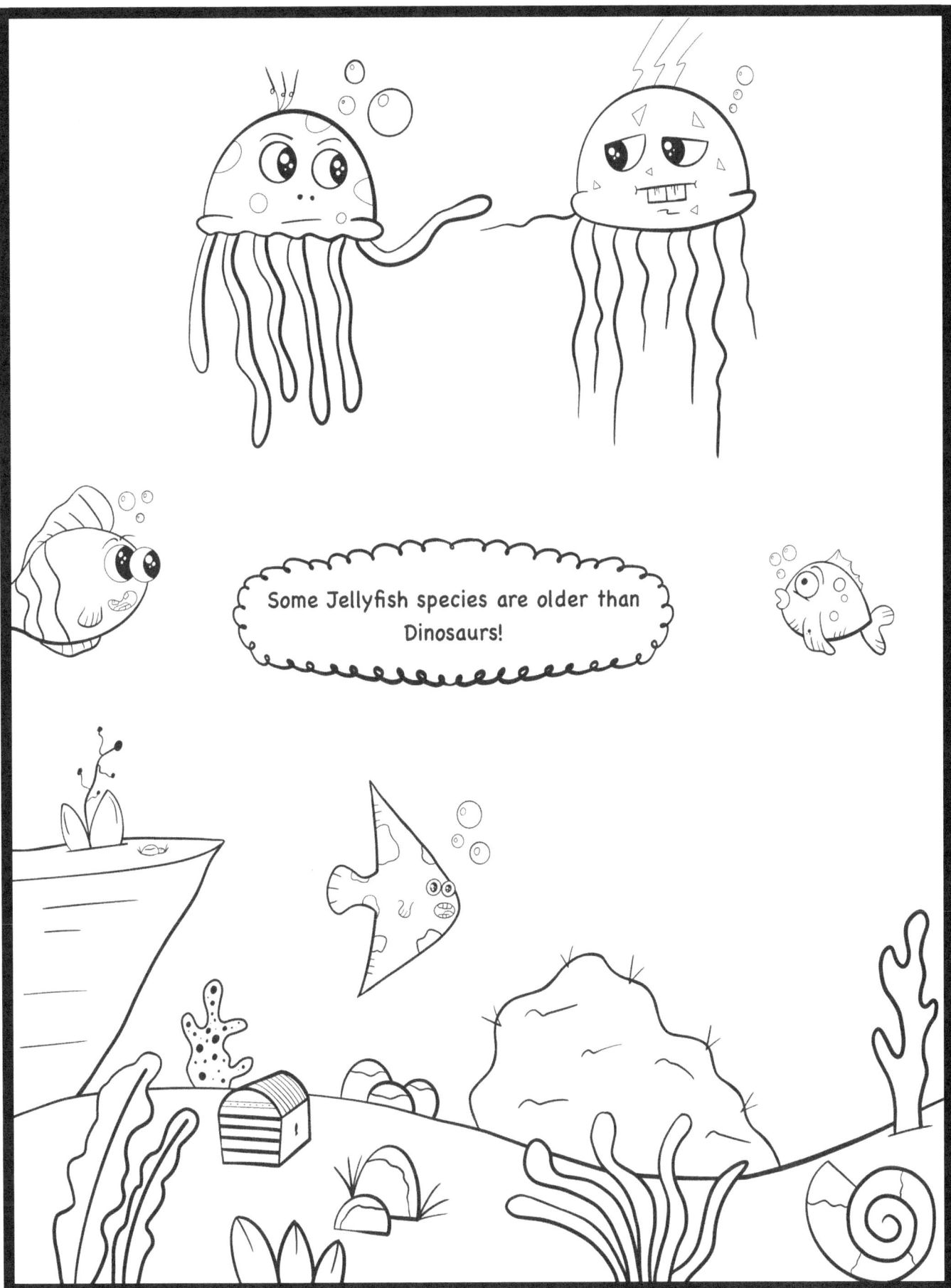

Jellyfish Challenge

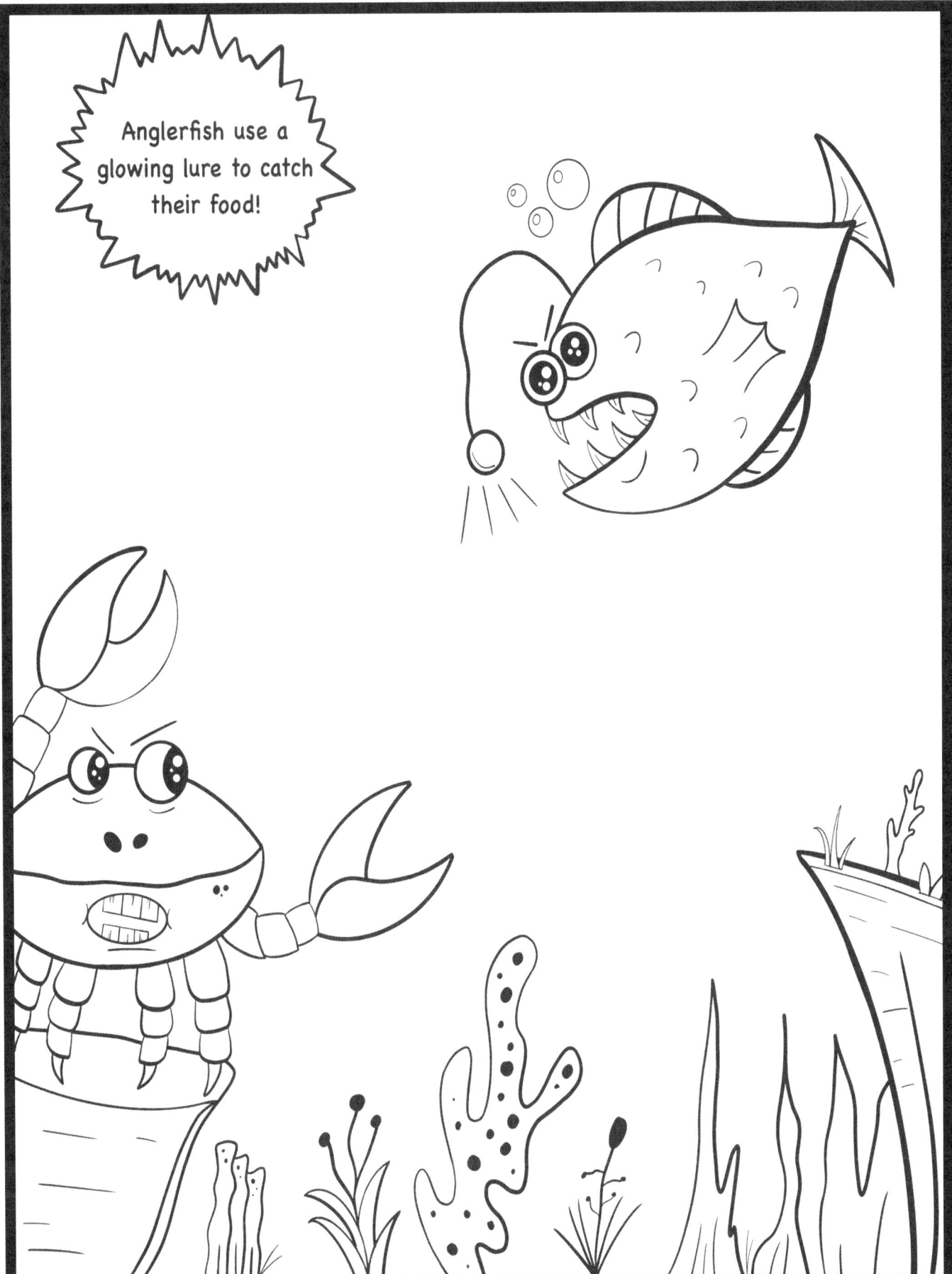

Bossy Anglerfish

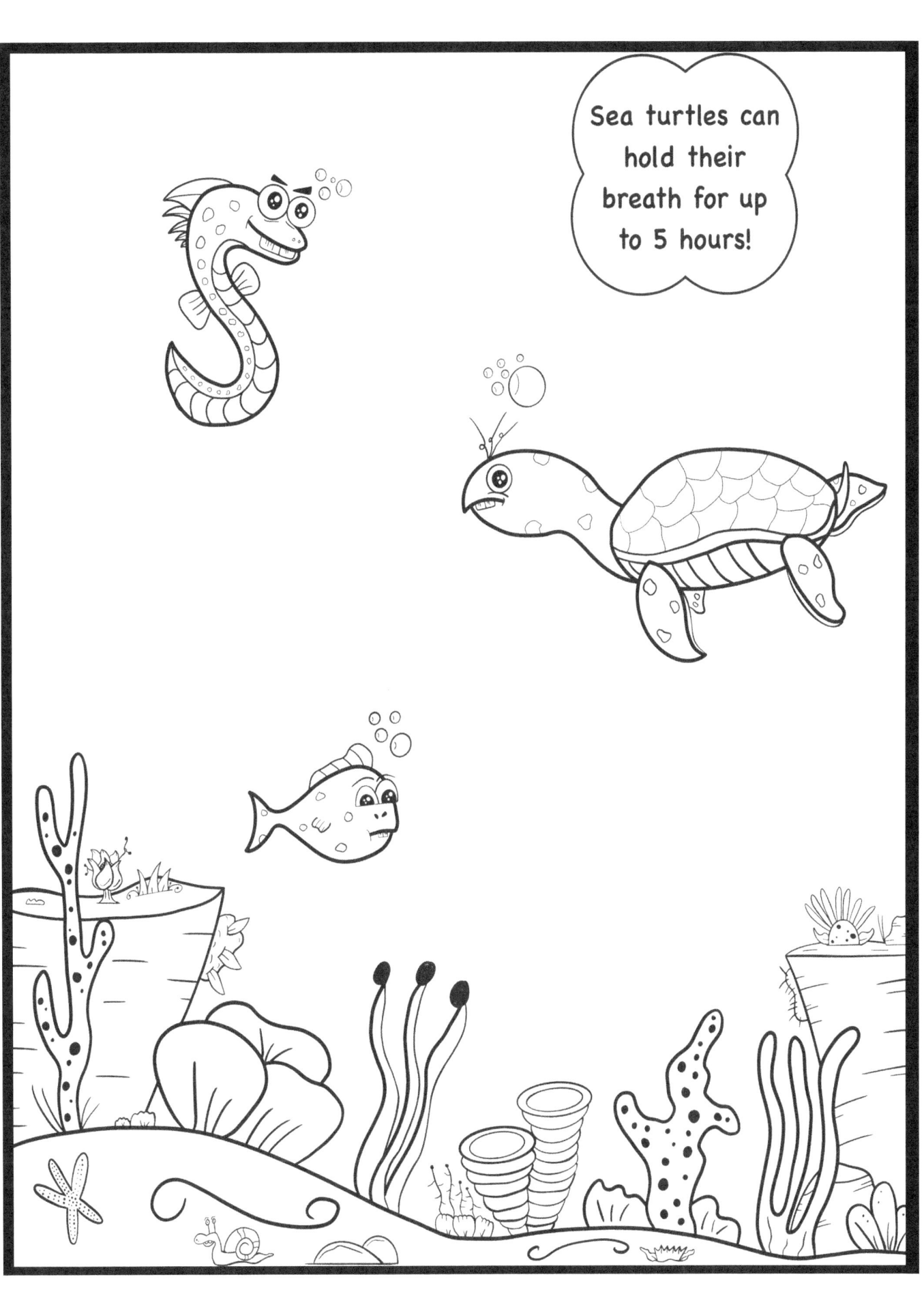

Confused Sea Turtle

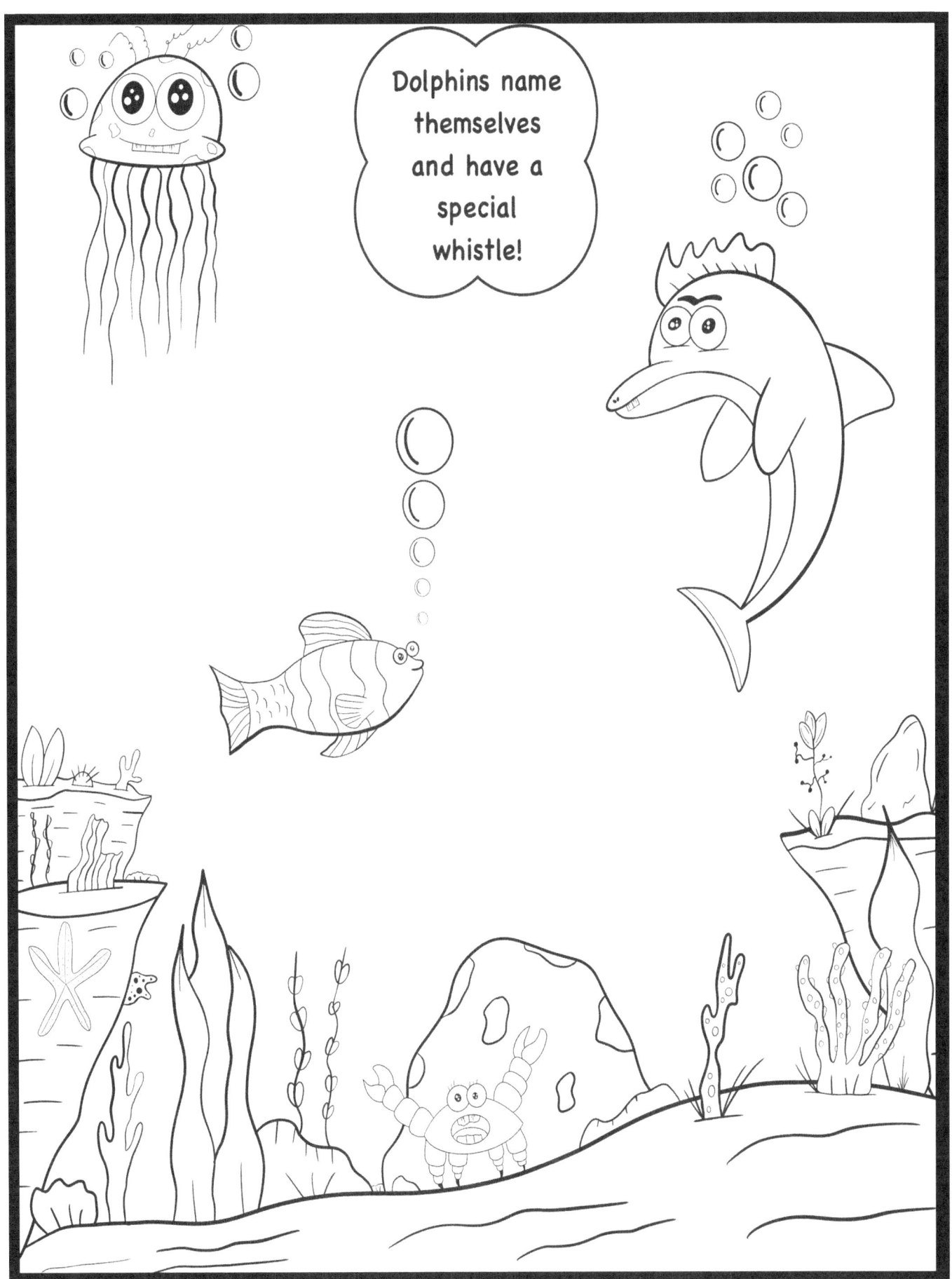

Spacey Dolphin

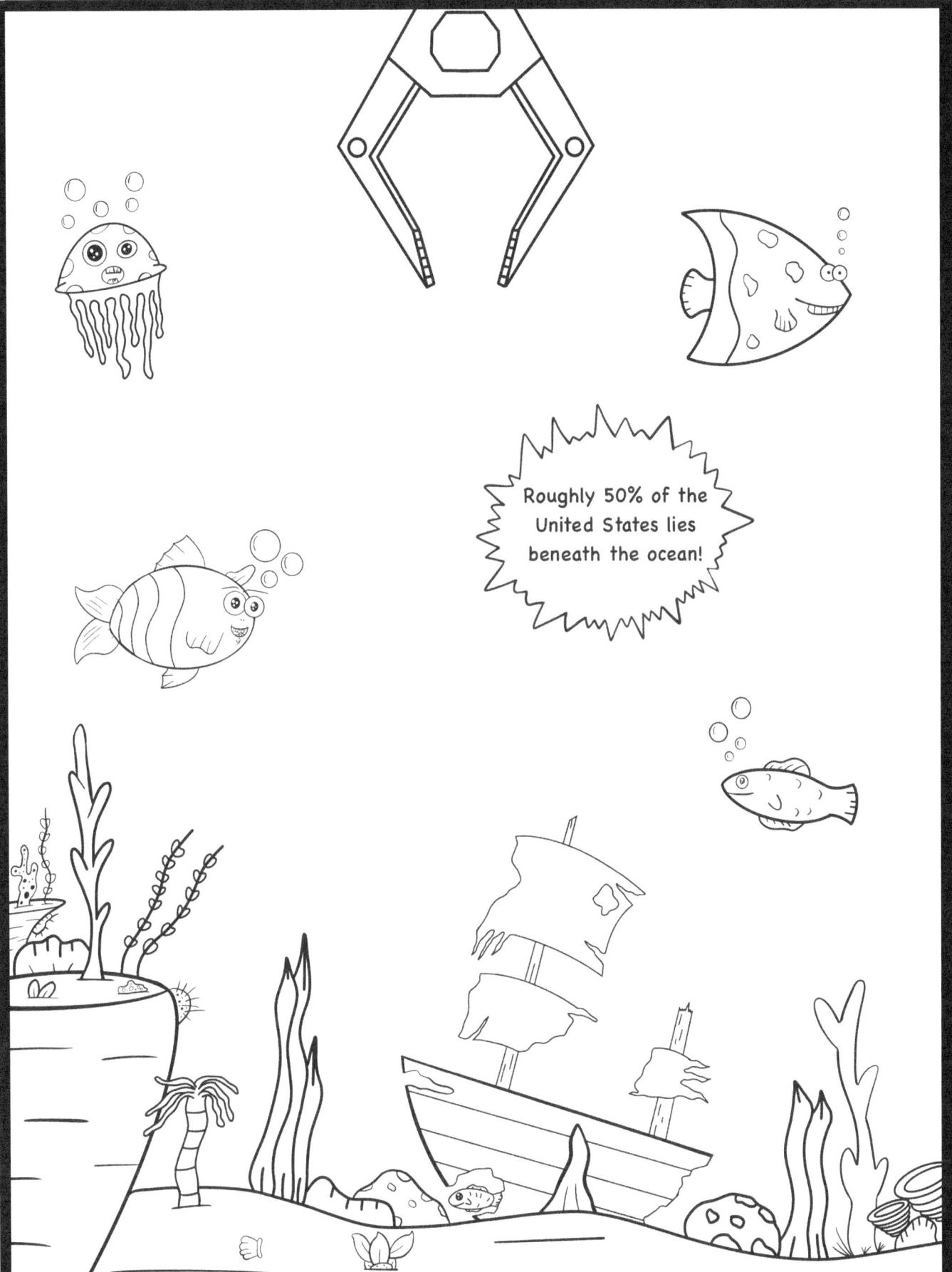

Sunken Ship

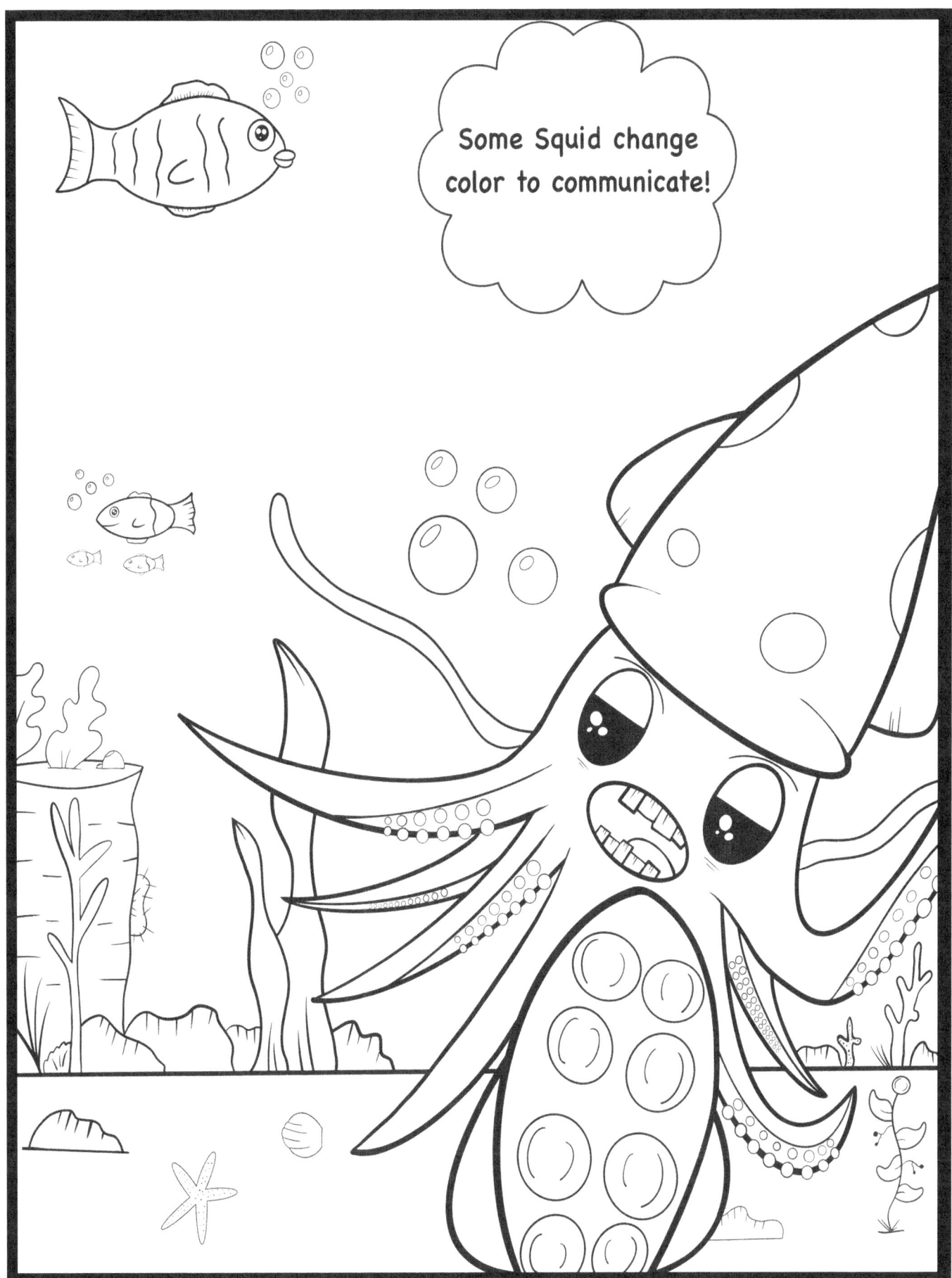

Giant Squid

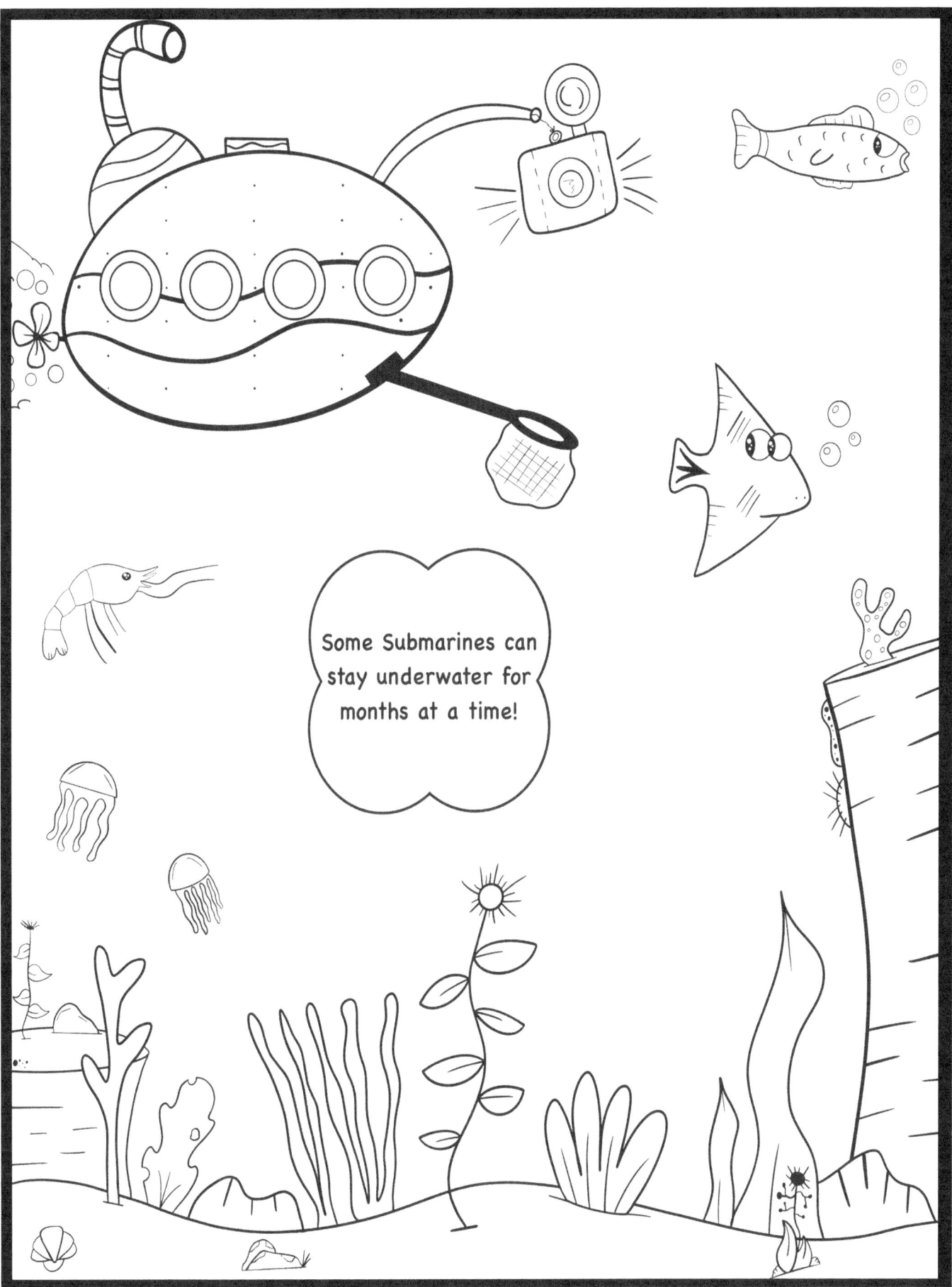

Submarine Adventure

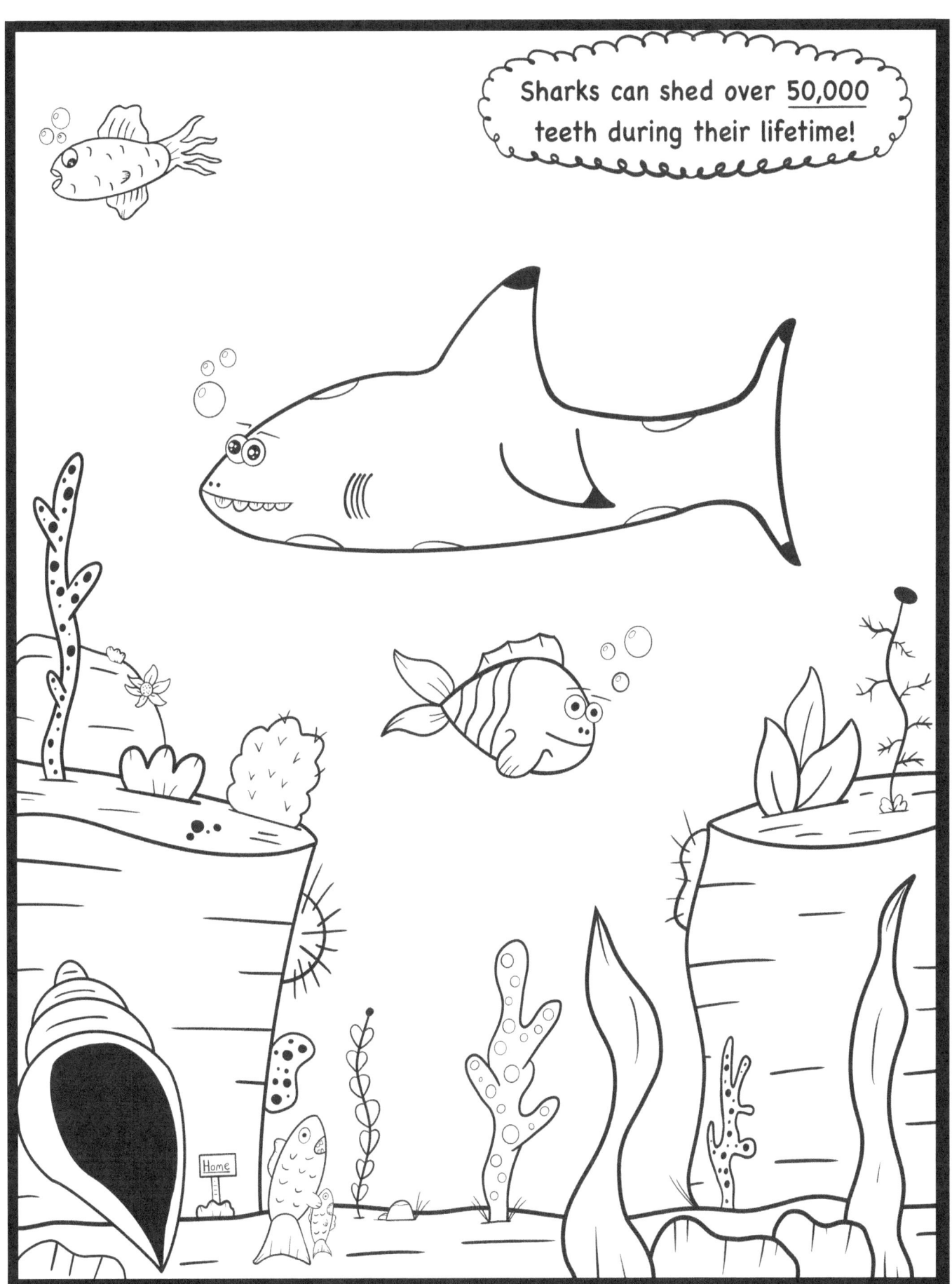

Shark Exhibit

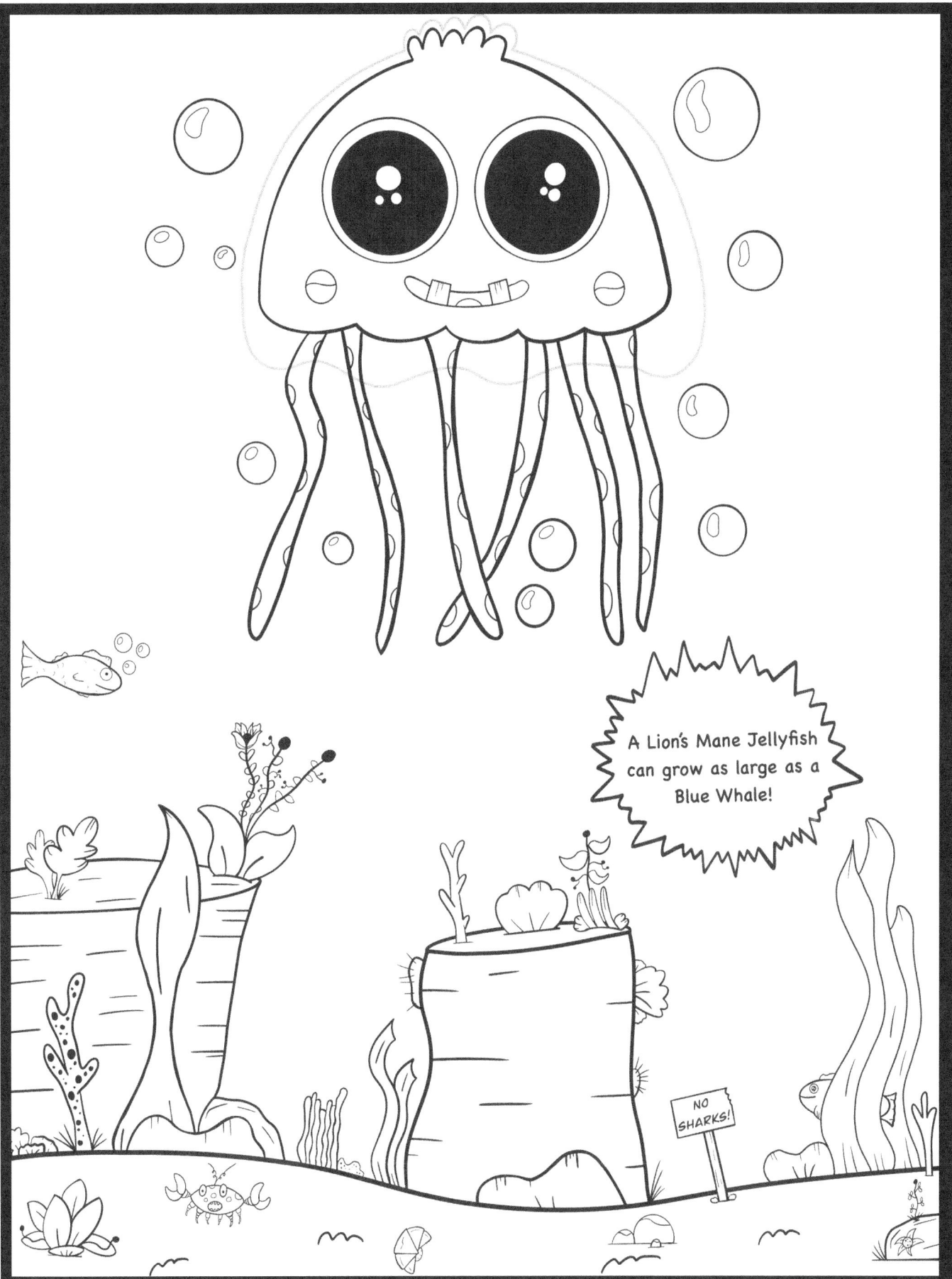

Cheerful Jellyfish

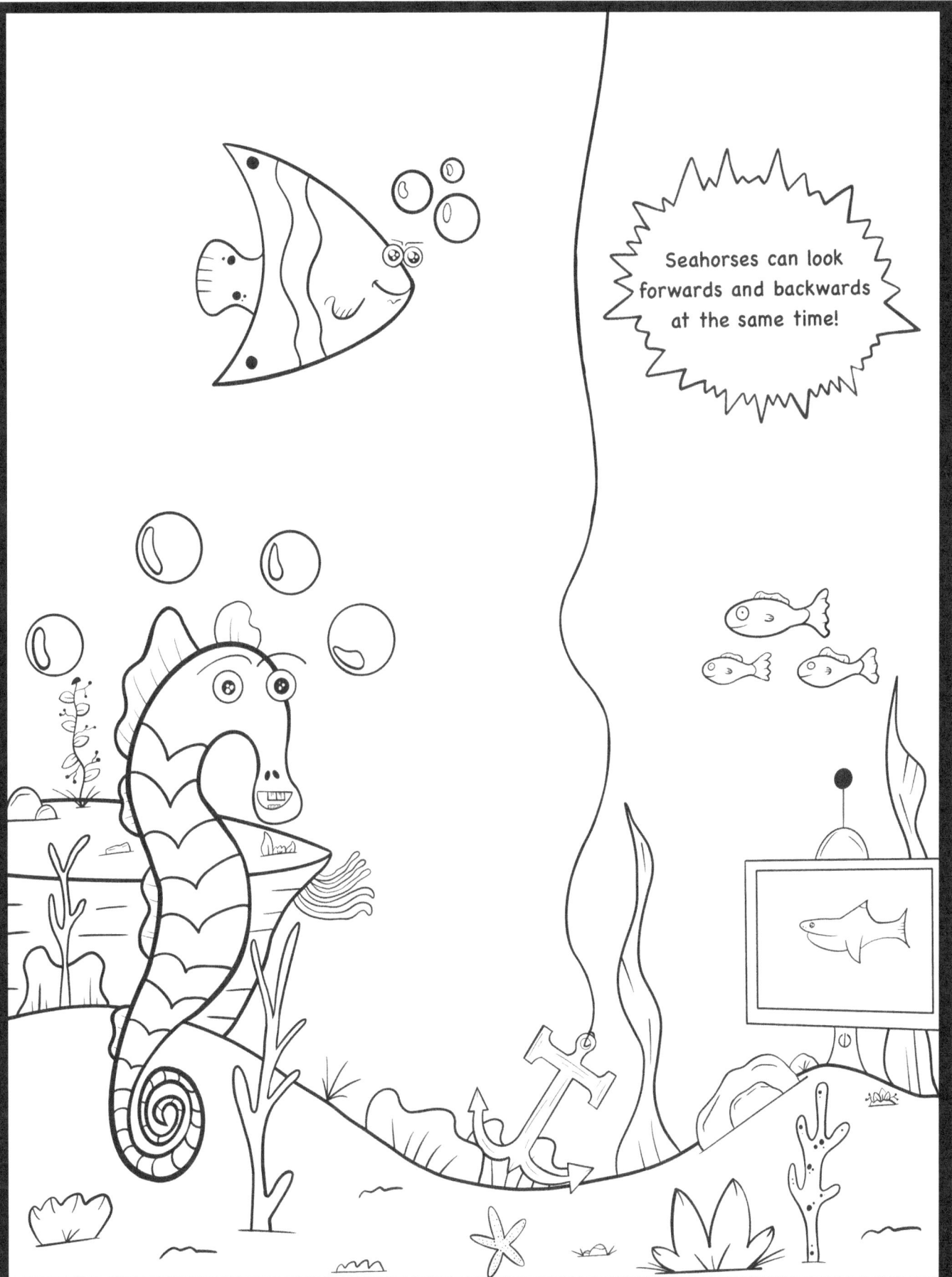

Seahorse Sanctuary

www.ingramcontent.com/pod-product-compliance
Lightning Source LLC
Chambersburg PA
CBHW060006230526
45472CB00008B/1965